Volume 1

Centered in Christ

Devotional

Steadfast and Immovable

JATNE Publishing™

Volume 1 Centered in Christ Devotional Steadfast and Immovable

Printed in the United States of America

Library of Congress Control Number: 2021920400

ISBN: 978-1-7320260-7-0

JATNE Publishing™

Writing Coach: Anna J. Small Roseboro

Editors: Tuesday Payne, Nikki West, Yolanda Whitehead

Book Cover Design: Nikki West

Spiritual -- Christian -- Daily Living -- Bible Study

TABLE OF CONTENTS

INTRODUCTION

Welcome and thank you for choosing to journey through this book of devotionals, the first in a Centered in Christ series. The theme for this devotional is" Steadfast and Immovable," which is not about being stiff or unwilling to move. Steadfast and immovable is about realizing that we all go through trials and tribulations, get off-track, and must come back to a place that is centered in Christ.

Paul encouraged the Corinthian church to remain faithful to everything he had taught them. To be steadfast and immovable is to be spiritually grounded. Thus, steadfast people know what they believe and need not be tossed back and forth, blown here and there by the winds and waves. As we learn to trust God, we become transformed into the predestined plan He has for our lives. He offers this call in his Word:

Therefore, my dear brothers and sisters, stand firm.

Let nothing move you.

Always give yourselves fully to the work of the Lord,

because you know that your labor in the Lord is not in vain.

1 Corinthians 15: 58 (NIV)

For this first volume of our Centered in Christ Devotional, Steadfast and Immovable, fifteen authors have taken time to write about their life experiences to show how they are fulfilling their work while trusting in the Lord. They share what they are learning to be steadfast and immovable, committed, firmly fixed, steady, and consistent for the Lord.

How to Use This Book

This book has several powerful devotionals and activities. The devotions are ideal for daily use, and for group discussion, or Bible study. Before beginning the book, take the time to pray to the Lord to reveal what He would have you get from these devotionals.

- Read each devotion.
- Respond to each prompt.
- Say the affirmation out loud. Go back to it throughout the day.
- Pray the prayer after each devotional. Make it personal.

BE A TEAM PLAYER

Sybil Davis-Highdale

Above all, love each other deeply because love covers

a multitude of sins. Offer hospitality to one another

without grumbling. Each of you should use whatever gift you have

received to serve others as faithful stewards

of God's grace in its various forms.

I Peter 4:8-10 (NIV)

So many things have changed in communities all over the world through the pandemic. People have become isolated; businesses and churches have closed their doors forever. There is one common denominator for all of us — we are crying for help. The body of believers needs each other and must learn to become a team, playing together. Let us examine the acronym of TEAM.

"T" talent is needed to be successful in meeting the needs of a hurting community. You must be willing to build on your God-given talents and passions. According to 1 Corinthians 12, God gave you gifts and a purpose to serve others. There can be no success without the development of talent. Natural talent indeed helps. Yet honing those talents will take you further.

No one can do everything perfectly, so "E" everyone is needed. God has equipped you to be a blessing with different experiences, cultures, and perspectives. You may be creative or logical, a great debater or an excellent speaker, or gifted in hospitality.

"A" is for application because talent and people mean nothing if not exercised. 2 Timothy 2:15, Nehemiah 3:28, and James 2:26 remind us that we need to work. It's what we do that makes the difference. Many people can do what's required, but few are willing to work. Being a team player means doing what's needed to make a difference.

Finally, to be a team player, your "M" matters. Motivation keeps you moving in the right direction. 1Peter 4:11 keeps us focused on the goal of God's true purpose and not on self or the praises of people.

No matter what goes on in this world, we must remember that we need each other. Without teamwork, little will be accomplished.

Respond Here

Think about and write down the dream(s) or vision(s) God has placed in your heart. Who can you bring alongside you to accomplish it as a team?

_____

_____

_____

_____

_____

Think about the team. What is your true motivation when activating your talents for the sake of others?

_____

_____

_____

_____

_____

Affirmation

God thank you for the gifts and talents You have blessed me with to apply it in building up the team, so we all are successful.

It's Praying Time

Father, I thank You for this opportunity to become a godly team player. Thank You for giving me purpose through this current assignment and the building blocks for the next. Transform me and strengthen me to submit to Your will to realize the needs of those I serve and be a blessing to those I work alongside. Lord, help me see the conditions and meet those needs to Your Glory.

In Jesus' Name, Amen

BE PERFECT

Jacqueline Smith

The Lord will perfect that which concerneth me:

thy mercy, O Lord, endureth forever:

forsake not the works of thine own hands.

Psalms 138:8 (KJV)

Be Perfect? With this word perfect, my mind immediately goes to trying to do something in a manner of perfection. But when I looked up the biblical meaning of the word perfect, what stood out was that God implies that to be perfected means mature, what is needful of me the most.

This process of being mature is a great challenge to us all in one way or another. It's hard to hear someone tell you to grow up when you think you are already grown. Developed in body, yet the mind has yet to mature in certain areas.

I remember when I was around fourteen years old. My mom and I were at a restaurant, and she saw me doing something un-seemly which embarrassed her. She did not expect me to do such a thing. She said to me, "Jackie, when are you going to grow up?"

To hear those words, even at the age of fourteen, hurt my feelings. Those words brought attention to where I had not grown. This feeling made me re-adjust my behavior.

Many do not want to hear the truth when they are in confusion. What we think and do becomes the basis of who we become. Our development depends upon various areas and what we have been allowed to do throughout our lives.

To be perfect or mature means that we can no longer behave like children. God wants to perfect us and mature us into his image.

Therefore, He allows us to make our own decisions, allowing happenstances to take place in our lives to perfect us in such a way that we can extend the grace that God bestowed to us upon others.

Respond Here

Think about and write what you believe God desires you to mature in. Share how you expect God to develop you towards perfection.

_____

_____

_____

_____

_____

God desires us to trust Him. Do you trust Him in the process? How can you be an example to others through this process?

_____

_____

_____

_____

_____

Affirmation

I will allow God to continue to perfect those things that I am concerned about even to my own hurt.

It's Praying Time

Lord, I give You praise today, for Your loving kindness towards me. You said that you would perfect those things that I am concerned about. You created me and designed me to fulfill Your divine destiny. I know that You will not forsake the works of Your hands, for I am Your workmanship, everything about me was formed by Your hands and Your hands alone has orchestrated my life. Therefore, I yield myself unto You that Your highest will be done in my life. Thank you, Father, for Your love toward me, and Your bountifully blessings that You have bestowed upon me. Lord, You are worthy to be praised.

In Jesus' Name, Amen

BE STILL AND TRUST GOD

Dr. Irene Watson

Be still, and know that I am God:

I will be exalted among the heathen,

I will be exalted in the earth.

Psalm 46:10 (KJV)

Memories of my childhood weekends come to mind as I think of being still and trusting God through life's processes. Visions of my mother pressing my sisters' and my hair every Saturday evening in a small, crowded kitchen become vivid. The smell of Sunday dinner cooking and the sounds of my mother's favorite blues songs ring in my ears as if it were yesterday. Obeying when I heard my mother say, "Be still, girl, and wait. I'll be finished in a minute," was the hardest thing for me to do.

Although my mother was a hairstylist and an expert with the hot iron, my body would shrink when it was my turn. The closer it got to my turn to sit in her styling chair, the more my mind would wrestle with wanting to run away and hide. Anyone who's ever had their hair hot-ironed probably understands where I'm coming from; it's not the most comfortable experience.

My mother would say, "Be still and wait." I hear God's voice saying, "Be still and know," when I am troubled and become impatient on those rough days in my life. When life becomes overwhelming with unending pain in my body and a mind that feels like shutting down, I must stay focused to continue forward.

I have learned that being still in the presence of God is quite different than sitting in that styling chair praying for the moment to end. As an adult, being still has become a "motionless rhythm of my mind," a time of intimacy that surpasses the carnal mind. It is a time of hope where everything is laid at God's altar in surrender.

Time alone with God has taught me to be still and know Him personally through His Word. Just as I trusted and believed in my mother's words of assurance, I now have greater trust in my Heavenly Father that His Word will come to pass. As I stay in the Lord's presence, I consistently remind myself to be still and know that nothing is impossible with Him.

Respond Here

Give an example of a time when you believed God to answer a personal prayer request, and you had to wait on the Lord. Share how you felt when your prayer request was answered. If you are still waiting, list what you are doing to build your trust in this season of being still.

_____

_____

_____

_____

Think about a time when you had to be still during a personal, raging storm and trust God to see you through it. Share, a few things you did to keep you steady through your storm.

a. _____

_____

b. _____

_____

c. _____

_____

Affirmation

As I live under an open heaven of favor and protection, I am victorious, and growing stronger every day because my trust is in God.

It's Praying Time

Almighty God, be exalted in my life so that I may be a living expression of You on the earth. You are Lord over all people and things. Besides You, there is none other; be thou exalted among the nation and in the world. Let your glory fill the earth so that all men will know that You are God. I surrender my life to You, take control of all my affairs. Be magnified in my life Father God and give me the insight that I need to be still and see Your glorious power work within me.

In Jesus' Name, Amen

DIVINE RESTORATION

Camelia Grannum

For I know the plans I have for you," declares the Lord, "
plans to prosper you and not to harm you,
plans to give you hope and a future.
Then you will call upon me and come and pray to me,
and I will listen to you. You will seek me and find me
when you seek me with all your heart."
Jeremiah 29: 11-13 (NIV)

Growing up in a small town, I have sweet memories of narrow hilly roads, gorgeous starry nights, cows, and goats grazing in the yard. Going to church every Sunday was a way of life.

"Camellia, it's bedtime," Mom shouted from inside as I sat on the veranda waiting for my father.

"I am waiting for Daddy. He said he was coming, and I can't sleep until he comes." I was ten years old, "He promised," I muttered with tears streaming down my cheeks.

"Go to bed. Don't you see it's late!" my mom said in a tone of frustration.

Unfortunately, my dad didn't show up that night; he didn't call. I was hurt and disappointed once again. As I prayed to ease the pain in my heart, God showed up when I needed Him the most. Prayer made the difference.

"Don't I matter?" I cried out. "Why does no one care about me? I want to understand and be understood." As I vented my frustrations and sufferings sobbing, my mom charged in angry, scolding me again to get inside. I asked her, "Can't I wait for just a bit longer?" She said okay.

Suddenly I heard a still small voice whispering in my heart, "Beloved, peace be still." At that moment everything was good. Instantly I felt love, safety, fearlessness, joy, and many more emotions flooded my soul.

Reflecting on this experience with my mother has caused me to be more aware of how my choices, words, and actions affect my children. I desire to guard their hearts.

Love is a choice, so I choose to be the love I desperately wanted for myself growing up. God showed up for me when no one else would. In my most vulnerable state. He restored my soul, giving me the gifts of grace and unconditional love.

Respond Here

God restores lives. Share an experience, or a time when you saw God moving in your life and He restored you from a situation or circumstance.

_____

_____

_____

_____

Share three ways you can ensure you are making the right choices in your life? Keep in mind that our choices affect everyone around us, and we must live with our choices.

a. _____

_____

b. _____

_____

c. _____

_____

Affirmation

I am strong, bold, and loved as a child of a King, and I know
He is never too busy for me.

It's Praying Time

Father, I feel safe in Your presence; You are the rock on which I
stand. My foundation, one that can never be broken, is
steadfast and immovable. Show me how to love selflessly.
Grant me the discernment to see the good in others and show
forgiveness. Thank You for your deliverance and the strength
to push through the challenges of life. Help me to live in unity
and love. May I walk in the light and spread the light to others.
Help me be great at demonstrating to our children what it truly
means to be a parent. Help me make responsible choices and be
an agent of love, change, and unity.

In Jesus' Name, Amen

DIVORCED FROM MY FEARS

Paulette Jaminson

For God hath not given us the spirit of fear

but of power and of love

and of a sound mind

2 Timothy 1:7 (KJV)

I can remember clearly the bright sunny day I got out of bed observing nothing familiar. Scanning the room, the one face I searched for was missing. I had left Kingston, Jamaica and moved to London when I was five years old. A tall, fair-skinned lady, my unknown grandmother, said, "Hello, come here. Are you hungry?" I did not answer, my heart beating fast, anxiously awaiting my mother to enter the room.

"Where is she? I want her." She is all I could imagine. Devastated, I concluded she had vanished. I cried aloud in desperation. No one could comfort me. It was my first head-on collision, hit by fear.

I did not play with the other children much; I loved being in my grandmother's garden. My favorite flowers were the yellow and red ones. Touching them reminded me of my mother's soft hands on my face. The reality was each day in the garden, fear kept creeping into my spirit. The words "she is not coming back" started my relationship with fear, and eventually, we got married.

Three years ago, I was diagnosed with breast cancer. I had a fear of cancer because two cousins had previously died from lung cancer. When I got the call from the doctor giving the results, I stopped, dropped, and prayed. I prayed and read scriptures that revealed to me that my marriage to fear was illegal.

God is bigger than cancer, and He is more significant than anything that we fear. The question is, "How do we overcome fear?" I believe there are three ways: praying in faith, speaking in faith, and doing in faith. Faith grows when we use it, or we will lose it.

For five months, I went through the entire cancer treatment process, experiencing minimal side effects. There was not one day that I could not get out of bed. The faith I had in God helped me not to bend, shake, or break. He was and still is my power source.

Although fear will arise, I choose to be no longer married to fear, and I choose faith, trusting in God through it all.

Respond Here

Write a few steps that will help to strengthen your faith when faced with fear.

a. _____

_____

b. _____

_____

c. _____

_____

From reading the devotion what can you do to ensure you are choosing joy over happiness?

_____

_____

_____

_____

Affirmation

I will walk in the power of faith and commit to conquer my fears daily.

It's Praying Time

Lord, I thank You for being the great I am, the King of Kings and the Lord of Lords, the creator of Heaven and Earth. I thank you for Your promise never to leave me or forsake me. Lord, I know Your promise is my shield and my protection. Lord, help me to decide to walk by faith when I am faced with fears. I decree and declare today I am delivered from the stronghold of fear in my life.

In Jesus' Name, Amen

DON'T PRAY AND WORRY

Nikki West

Jesus replied, "Truly I tell you if you have faith
and do not doubt, not only can you do what was done
to the fig tree, but also you can say to this mountain,
'Go, throw yourself into the sea,' and it will be done."

Matthew 21:21 (NIV)

The statement "don't pray and worry" is one that I had heard for many years. However, it was easier said than done. I was a person who grew up in the church but was still what one would call "ye of little faith." Don't get me wrong. I didn't feel like I had little faith; my inability to have unwavering faith showed others something completely different.

Here I was, 30 years old, and deciding to go back to college. I had a husband and three children, two under the age of five, and a job. The two youngest were one and three. My husband was active-duty military. We lived in California, but he was deployed. Let me point out that my family, my support system, was all on the East Coast.

I started college when I graduated from high school but wasn't ready and wasted time and money. Once I was prepared to go back to school, I was derailed again by marriage and babies. Now, I was determined to finish college, asking God to keep me sane. In addition to sanity, I prayed for confidence and the ability to stay on task.

Of course, I was nervous and more worried than I should have. I had moments where I pulled my hair, screamed, and might have lost my mind while writing a paper, but God always answered and had my back. I made it through the deployment, kept my job, raised my children, made a military move across the United States, and finished my degree.

Every night I would sing Mary Mary's "Can't Give Up Now," which helped me keep my focus. Those words kept me going. They reminded me that even when I felt like I couldn't take it anymore, God was always there for me to lean on.

After three and a half years, I walked across the stage. My husband and children cheering me on and a GPA over 3.0. Worry was just a trick that the devil was playing on me. Through it all, I learned an essential process – to always pray and not worry.

Respond Here

Write about a time that you had to turn your doubt from fear to fulfill what you set out to do.

_____

_____

_____

_____

Think back to a time when you prayed but still worried? Was your prayer answered and do you think worry delayed the answer?

_____

_____

_____

_____

Affirmation

I will pray without worry or doubt, always remembering that God is with me and has my back.

It's Praying Time

Father God, how I love and thank You for all that You've done for me. Help me to remember that belief and doubt are both verbs, and doubt does not mean my faith has failed. I need Your help to settle my heart and mind so that I may endure to the end. I present my body as a living sacrifice, holy, acceptable, and pleasing in Your sight. I repent for letting my thoughts run wild and thank You for loving me despite my overactive thoughts and occasional doubt.

In Jesus' Name, Amen

FROM TEARS TO LAUGHTER

Lekeisha Mosley

Sarah said, "God has brought me laughter,

and everyone who hears about this

will laugh with me."

Genesis 21:6 (KJV)

The word laughter brings freedom to mind. Playing outside and racing to get home before the streetlights came on at 8:00 p.m. was my idea of freedom when I was ten years old. At age 30, I would smile and laugh, thinking about how my childhood was carefree.

Often, I recall wondering if others expressed themselves in the same way when thinking back on their childhood. Several of my colleagues shared that there was too much work to do than thinking about laughing and childhood memories. I was saddened, realizing that everyone didn't feel the same way about being carefree.

There was a movie called *Up* (2009), and in the film, 78-year-old Carl Frederickson is about to fulfill a lifelong dream and complete a promise made to his late wife, Ellie. She had dreams for herself and her husband, Carl, to fly across the world. Saving and losing their funds, they both began to believe that their goals would never happen.

Ellie passes away, leaving her husband knowing their dreams of flying to South America are still undone. Carl becomes strong, knowing work is required to complete their journey.

Carl packs and prepares to leave. On the journey, he realized there is onboard a young male, Russell, a stowaway. With this unexpected twist, he continues to enjoy his journey to fly to South America with Russell. They befriend each other, and Carl becomes a mentor to Russell.

My experience reflecting on the movie *Up* inspired me to focus on my relationship with Christ first. Preparing myself in my workplace for those who need support and learning how to have the freedom of laughter.

Respond Here

When you hear the word laughter, what comes to mind? Share a time when you had a good laugh and how it made you feel.

_____

_____

_____

_____

_____

Share what freedom means to you and how laughter fits to bring a smile to your face.

_____

_____

_____

_____

_____

Affirmation

Lord thank You for guiding me to never give up, or lose faith, but to stay hopeful and laugh through it all as I endure the ebb and flow in life.

It's Praying Time

Lord, how excellent You are in my life. I thank You for the great laughter you have given to me. Thank You that I now realize that I have the freedom to choose and joy. My heart is filled with joy as I think about Your greatness as the Rock of my Salvation. I magnify and glorify Your Righteous Name. Help me to daily live in You with a happy heart to share with others. Guide my thoughts so that they are pleasing to You. I pray that all will seek You so that they may find joy unspeakable joy. The joy that no one can give, to them, and no one can take it away.

In Jesus' Name, Amen

GOD WILL SEE YOU THROUGH

Noreen Hobson

For with God nothing shall be impossible.

Luke 1:37 (KJV)

Have you ever dealt with a situation or problem where you felt like the weight of the world was on your shoulders? Here I was working a full-time job, pregnant and preparing with my husband to welcome our second bundle of joy into our family when I was downsized.

The reality was I had no job and no health insurance. To make matters worse, a global pandemic, COVID-19, had just broken out, and not only was I going through a challenging personal situation, but now so was the whole world.

The stress of tirelessly looking for health insurance was exhausting. It is often said when life gives you lemons, make lemonade. So how could a problem turn around and become sweet? The answer is God.

I stopped trying to resolve my problems myself and instead sought the Power of God to make a way. I prayed sincerely and earnestly to God for help. I was amazed to receive health insurance the same month the baby was to be born. My prayers were answered just in the nick of time.

God restored and multiplied what I had lost. Months later, I was able to launch out by Faith and LevelUp My Career to a higher position. Overall, God turned what I had perceived as a challenging situation into a blessing.

Through this, I learned to go to God first, ask Him for help and seek His perspective daily. The lemons of life do not compare to the blessed sweet assurance of Jesus Christ to see me through any situation.

In the end, my faith in God strengthened, my love for Christ became further centered, steadfast, and immovable as I remembered that there's nothing God can't see me through. Give your problems to Jesus; He cares.

Respond Here

Think and write about a situation you need to pray and trust God to see you through. Remember, God can do the impossible. Luke 1:37 (KJV)

_____

_____

_____

_____

_____

Share a few lessons you learned and, what characteristics developed when putting God first in your life.

_____

_____

_____

_____

Affirmation

I believe God and trust Him with my whole heart and will not try

figure it out on my own, but trust and know You will direct my path.

It's Praying Time

Glory to God, the Father of everything. Thank You, for giving me this day to praise and honor You. I can do nothing on my own if not for Your loving kindness, tender mercy, and grace in my life. Thank You for divine guidance in everything I do, everywhere I go, and in everything I say. I present my needs and my situation before you Lord and ask your will God to be done. Keep me in perfect peace and of a sound mind. Help me to remember that there is nothing impossible with You and nothing too big that you can't solve. Thank you, Jesus Christ, my Savior, and Holy Spirit for your direction. I surrender myself to you, God. Let my life be a blessing and bless me today.

In Jesus' Name, Amen

HE SAID, "YES!"

Neva Brooks

For no matter how many promises God has made,

they are "Yes" in Christ. And so through him

the "Amen" is spoken by us to the glory of God.

2 Corinthians 1:20 (NIV)

I remember when my fiancé popped the question: "Will you marry me?" While I was trying to get myself together, he got down on one knee, opened that little black ring box with a breathtaking diamond, and I said, "YES!" He was so excited, and he told everyone who would listen, "Hey y'all, she said YES!"

Even though the promises of my marriage did not last, I know the promises of God are YES and forever, Amen.

`God gently whispered reminders of His promises to lead and provide for me. As a new entrepreneur, I was stuck and overwhelmed in trying to put it all together. I paused to reevaluate my progress and lack thereof. I said, "God, am I really on track with what you said?" He led me to 2 Corinthians 1:20, the focus scripture for this devotional.

I researched a bit further and realized there are over 3,000 God-given promises in the Bible. With each of these promises comes a "Yes" and an "Amen" to the glory of God through us. That means we must participate!

First, we must ensure that our lives are in alignment with the words of God in His promises. Next, we must receive His promises in the name of Jesus, the Amen.

God gave us the true Lord and Savior, whose name is Jesus Christ. God's promises are made complete in Christ. When our plans seem to be derailed by the everyday problems of life, we can refer to the promises of God and agree to His promises to the Glory of God.

Open the Bible and the box of God's eternal promises, trust and believe His promises are freely available. Align your life with His promises and the next time you aren't feeling confident, remember His promises are forever, and you too can shout to all who will listen, "Hey y'all, He said, "YES!" It is so! Amen.

Respond Here

What is the number one area of your life you are willing to align with a promise of God?

_____

_____

_____

_____

List two steps you can take to respond to God's promises.

a. _____

_____

b. _____

_____

Affirmation

I know He will supernaturally give provision for his promises, because when Jesus say's "YES", nobody can say NO!

It's Praying Time

Father You are the Only True and Living God and I simply adore You! I believe Your promises are YES and Amen and You are the ultimate promise keeper! I thank You for sending Your son Jesus Christ who fulfills your words. Forgive me for ever doubting Your faithfulness toward me. I will continue to focus and refocus on Your Holy Scriptures. Thank you for leading me to the authority and power in Your promises. I pray that everyone who reads Your promises will believe them, trust the truth in them, and align their lives to Your promises for Your glory.

In Jesus' Name, Amen

I SURRENDER ALL

Cynthia Crawford

Trust in the Lord with all your heart

and lean not on your own understanding.

In all your ways submit to him,

and he will make your paths straight.

Proverbs 3:5-6 (NIV)

God provided an opportunity for me to step into a deeper relationship with Him one Thursday afternoon in September 2020. Several stressful situations surrounded me. The COVID-19 pandemic altered everyday life. Unrest continued from the racial injustice witnessed during the George Floyd murder, and politics further divided the nation as the presidential election approached. Amidst all this, cancer reemerged in my mother's body.

These compounding circumstances reached a crescendo on this day. I tried to remain strong but felt on the verge of breaking. I stared out the glass of my front door, observing the view for a moment of relief. In my gaze, a single heart-shaped leaf on the porch captivated my attention with its fragility exemplified against the hardness of the concrete; its delicate nature allowed it to rest on the firm foundation.

The Holy Spirit used this illustration to gently challenge my perspective of exhibiting strength. My default posture resembled the concrete, remaining stoic no matter what came my way. Could I be strong and look like the leaf? Yes! The design of God's love for me provides Christ as my foundation, strengthening me when I surrender all to Him.

This divine display reminded me His ways are not like my ways. I did not understand the purpose of these health and social hardships that left me emptied. But I accepted the need to change my position of strength and give these burdens to Jesus.

I leaned on Him through prayer and stood on the unshakeable Word. This surrender filled my void with the Holy Spirit and empowered me to wholeheartedly believe, trust, and obey Jesus. My submission let me walk by faith through this darkness with Him guiding me. I'm now seeing the dawning of new things He is doing through me. His grace is sufficient.

Respond Here

Reflect on a hardship that brought you closer to God. What did you have to surrender to Him through Jesus?

_____

_____

_____

_____

Read Proverbs 3:5-6 from this devotional. List the things you must do to stand in the Lord?

a. _____

_____

b. _____

_____

c. _____

_____

Affirmation

I will believe, trust, and obey that God will make a way, working things out for my good.

It's Praying Time

Heavenly Father, thank You for who You are! Thank You for sending Jesus to save me, and now I have salvation in You. I am grateful that nothing can separate me from this love You have for me. I am in awe that You have chosen me to carry out the plans that You predestined for me. And because You have chosen me, I am qualified, flaws and all. In my weakness, help me to remember the power I have within me through the Holy Spirit. May I never take for granted what my salvation provides me. I surrender all to You, enabling everything You want to do in and through me to be done.

In Jesus' Name, Amen

LAY PROSTRATE

Dr. Annette West

Going a little farther,

he fell with his face to the ground and prayed,

"My Father, if it is possible,

may this cup be taken from me.

Yet not as I will, but as you will."

Matthew 26:39 (KJV)

Standing in my kitchen, I stare out the window, mentally rewinding to a tough season in my life. So many seasons. In this one, I had been ready to throw in the towel on my marriage. It had been a good day at the job. Then, to choir practice, I went. Oh, my goodness! It was high time. The choir elevated in pure worship before the Lord.

However, when I returned home, what hit me shook my world. That high dissipated quickly. It took everything within me to keep my composure. Yes, I felt a headache coming on as fumes flowed from my ears — or so it seemed.

My mind was racing. Do I see a woman in my house that does not belong? Stay focused, under control. Don't act out the children are watching. In my head, I hear, "Let me fight this battle."

I have learned to seek the Lord when something tough and unexpected rises. To lay prostrate before Him—knowing that He will always be with me in my daily relationship with Him.

So, amid this mental nightmare, I reverenced God, taking my thoughts from the situation at hand, choosing to be joyful amid the mess.

As portrayed in the devotional scripture, a person must fall, lay with their face to the ground. To be prostrate is a position of yielding in worship with a willingness to cry out to the Lord. In the facedown position, worship and prayer are essential in a heart connection with the Lord. Submission of the will, with no questions asked.

Enjoyment of His presence is what we gain when we fall, prostrate before Him. His presence, His Shekinah Glory, is magnified. The discipline to lay before the Lord is essential daily, preparing one for when tough times come.

Had I not been in an intimate daily relationship with the Lord standing through that season would have been unbearable. Being steadfast and immovable in the Lord is what kept me.

Respond Here

Think about a time you went through a rough season and knew the Lord was the only one to get you through. Write how you felt at that time and what you did to get through.

_____

_____

_____

_____

Think about and write what a daily relationship in the Lord means to you?

_____

_____

_____

_____

Affirmation

I will daily prostrate before the Lord to gain strength to sustain me in all situations.

It's Praying Time

Lord, how excellent You are in my life. Your Shekinah Glory fills this place as I bask in Your presence. I thank You for daily allowing me to come before Your throne. No matter the obstacles that arise, I know You are with me. I choose to lay before You daily, expecting Your presence to flow in my soul. I magnify and glorify Your Righteous Name. I worship You and recall that my purpose is to love and serve You first. Remaining steadfast and immovable in You is necessary for peace and joy to guide me.

In Jesus' Name, Amen

LIFE IS MY GIFT

Tuesday Payne

I shall not die, but live,

and declare the work of the Lord.

Psalm 118:17 (KJV)

It started small. Yet, with every passing hour, the pain increased so much that my head felt as if it would explode. I don't know when it began, yet it did. I woke up that morning in pain but pressed on despite how I felt.

Time was short, with lots to do before heading to work. Showering and dressing were challenging. How I made it to work at the nursing home, I do not know. It was as if I was watching someone else drive my car, but I was behind the wheel. I made it but only to fall on the sofa drenched in sweat. Paramedics arrived to assess the situation. Sirens blaring, to the hospital I went.

Test one – no dye. Test two with dye–not good news. "I am sorry to inform you the scan shows a brain bleed," says the doctor.

"What, a stroke?" That can't be. I thought it was just an excruciating migraine, but not so.

Over and over, I cried out, "I shall not die, but live, and declare the works of the Lord."

My God has brought me through many health issues. So, with a surety, I knew deliverance would come to me again. Hours passed from morning till night. Yet, in that time, I continued to walk by faith, not by what they saw. After they ran the major test, the neurologist called over the intercom, "Mrs. Payne, I don't see the bleed, it's gone." As I lay on that table, I shouted, "Hallelujah, my God is amazing." I prayed, "Father God, I thank You for not allowing the enemy to take my life."

Please know that no matter what you face, Jehovah God is more than able to see you through it. Stay encouraged in the Lord.

Respond Here

Recall a time in your life when you didn't seek the Lord when you knew you should have? What was the outcome of not seeking the Lord?

_____

_____

_____

_____

List a few ways the Scripture for this devotion ministers to you when you are ill and seeking healing.

a. _____

_____

b. _____

_____

c. _____

_____

Affirmation

My life is not my own; therefore, I will thank God daily for my life and, I will praise Him for His goodness, His mercy, and His grace.

It's Praying Time

My Father and my God, thank You for caring and loving me. Thank You, Father, that you never turn your back on me but show me brand new mercies every day. You are magnificent in all Your ways, and I am genuinely grateful that You called me as Your own. You have given me an unfailing love, an everlasting love that I do not deserve and am not worthy of, but I thank You that You are no respecter of person, and if you did it for me, You would surely do it for someone else. Thank You for keeping me and for never leaving me. You are the rock of my salvation, and in You, I stand strong and firmly rooted.

In Jesus' Name, Amen

MOVING INTO THE NEXT ASSIGNMENT

Sybil Davis-Highdale

Still, another said, "I will follow you, Lord, but first,

let me go back and say goodbye to my family."

Jesus replied, "No one who puts a hand to the plow

and looks back is fit for service

in the kingdom of God."

Luke 9:61-62 (NIV)

When thinking of the phrase "next assignment," a person may get fearful about the unknown or become depressed about all they'll have to leave behind, but not me. I've experienced ministry or military moves every two to five years almost my entire life. I've loved every place I've ever lived and have met great people learning invaluable lessons each time.

When I was ten, I couldn't understand why God could want me to leave family, but God never asks us to abandon anyone, instead give them to Him. When we hold on to people, things, and knowledge, we cannot embrace what's yet to come.

In the Bible, Moses went through four assignments. David transitioned from shepherd to warrior to king. Paul went from persecutor to apostle to writer. None of them would've reached God's purpose without following Him through assignments.

My experiences have led me into many assignments — family, military member, instructor, advisor, biker, missionary, pastor — the list goes on. I had no choice in some assignments and others that, if I'd hesitated, would've been lost, making me unprepared for the next. Each taught me new lessons and made me more valuable to my community and more marketable.

Degrees prove we're teachable, but experiences through new assignments make us usable for the more significant.

Jesus wasn't telling us to follow Him to be worthy. He was telling us to follow Him to witness God is worthy. In every assignment, see the greatness of God as He packs our toolboxes with gifts, talents, knowledge, and wisdom. God gives us every tool, but we get those tools on assignments.

Respond Here

What are your gifts, and/ or passions? How have you developed them in your current assignment?

_____

_____

_____

_____

List a few things you can do in the next six months to position yourself in obedience to God in pursuit of your next assignment?

a. _____

_____

b. _____

_____

c. _____

_____

Affirmation

Equipped and open, I will self-examine, learn, and grow as I walk into my next God-given assignment.

It's Praying Time

Thank You, Father, for grace and mercy. I praise You for all the assignments You have brought me through. I glorify You for choosing me for this journey. Father, give me the strength to step into my next assignment. Bless me with the courage to walk away from my past without looking back. Help me not to carry blame, guilt, or resentment into the future. Open the doors You have for me and lock the ones that are not part of Your plan. Give me the wisdom to know when You are leading. Open my eyes to see my next assignment before me. Open my heart to know who should walk with me in the next position and who and what I must leave in Your Hands.

In Jesus' Name, Amen

POSITIVITY IS KEY

Pablo Murillo

For as he thinketh in his heart, so is he:

Eat and drink, saith he to thee;

but his heart is not with thee.

Proverbs 23:7 (KJV)

I worked 30-hours, which made for a long week. A good thing is all my midterm exams were done, and I felt great. College life is busy, but Friday means time to relax. There is a party going on, and everyone will be there. I can go have some fun with my friends.

I get ready, put on my best clothes, comb my hair, put on some cologne in case I meet a young lady, and then right before I leave my bathroom, I look at myself in the mirror and say, "I wonder who I am going to mess up today?" Now you know back then, it was not "mess" that I said.

Every time I went anywhere, this was the similar routine I would go through during my college days. I was always wondering why other guys wanted to fight me all the time. I used to blame it on them, saying that they are player haters. They are just jealous of me, etc. I later realized that I was the energy, and everything I did was an energy exchange with others.

A singular thought about, maybe, the way someone looked at me could negatively impact my day. Then again, it really could have been anything.

The way I came into a room exemplified all the energy of that one thought and words I had uttered to myself, "They're just jealous!". Inevitably, other men in the room who had similar thoughts and energy would feel my presence and intent and would look my way. Once we saw each other, the rest became history. Our negative thoughts created negative energy and we were ready to fight with words and hands.

The Creator wrote in the Bible, "for a man thinketh so is he." Now that I have realized this powerful way of creating in my life, I have become mindful of how I think. I understand now that words have power, whether we say to the, ourselves or somebody else.

If you want an outstanding quality of life, begin by changing your thought process. Then the magic happens in your life with a positive mindset.

Respond Here

Think about a time that you were negative dealing with a person. Write your actions and your thoughts when you look back on it.

_____

_____

_____

_____

_____

List a few ways you can be positive every day.

a. _____

_____

b. _____

_____

c. _____

_____

Affirmation

I will daily keep my mind on positive thing that build up and leave negativity alone.

It's Praying Time

Thank you, Lord, for helping me to move from a daily negative mindset to a positive flow. I appreciate Your guiding me to be a better person and helping me to see my flaws. I trust Your promises in and over my life. Thank You for being the sacrifice that set me free from the bondage of sin. I thank You for this lovely life and the abundance of Your blessings. Thank You for Your continued grace and mercy, my faith in you daily increases. Your love is unmeasurable, and I trust You in all things.

In Jesus' Name, Amen

STANDING ON HIS PROMISES

Janice Rock

Let us hold unswervingly to the hope we profess,

for he who promised is faithful.

Hebrews 10:13 (NIV)

Have you heard the phrase, "Your word is your bond?" I have always believed those words to be true. Until proven otherwise, I will trust and believe your word. When someone makes a promise but does not come through, we become disappointed that they did not keep their word.

When I was a child, I looked forward to going to the county fair and riding the donkeys at the petting zoo. Every year, I would ask my dad, "Can we go to the fair?" I trusted and believed him, so all I needed was his word. If he said, "yes," I knew he would do everything in his power to honor his promise. My dad never disappointed me.

As I look back into the Word, I see that Christ made a promise to His children many years ago. He committed to sacrificing His life on the cross for the sins of the world. Regardless of the persecution He suffered, He remained focused and fulfilled His promise.

God's promises are a reassurance that He is with us through all that life may bring. It could be a negative report from the doctor, the loss of a job or death of a loved one, His promises remain yes and amen. He will not allow his word to falter or fail.

When God say's it, you can believe it will come to pass. He will help you fight every battle and to win every war. He is Abba, our Daddy/Father.

Respond Here

List three promises God had applied to your life.

a. _____

_____

b. _____

_____

c. _____

_____

Share one of God's promises that you believe is true daily for you? Explain why this promise is essential to you.

_____

_____

_____

_____

_____

Affirmation

I am standing on every promise you make Lord; I trust every word I hear you say, and I know it will come to pass.

It's Praying Time

Thank You, Lord, for your promises and the sacrifice You made to redeem us. You love me so much. Your only Son went to the cross and died a natural death so that I may have abundant life in You. Lord, Your word is a lamp unto my feet and a light unto my path. Your promises illuminate my life with beautiful blessings. I will declare Your promises daily and share the best of you with others. Because of Your grace and mercy, my faith and hope have increased. Your love is unmeasurable.

In Jesus' Name, Amen

THEN THERE WERE NONE

Nikki West

Do not be yoked together with unbelievers.

For what do righteousness and wickedness

have in common? Or what fellowship

can light have with darkness?

2 Corinthians 6:14 (NIV)

Some people grow up believing in fairy tales, excited for the day that they'll meet the person of their dreams and live 'happily ever after.' Over time, the reality sets in that it is not as easy as they thought.

At age 22, I was dating a guy I had been friends with for a couple of years. He was funny, listened to me, had excellent communication skills, educated, went to church, and loved his family. I was smitten and thought I had finally found my happily ever after. However, the relationship didn't last long.

It was a cool fall night, and we were at the park, lying on the hood of the car and looking at the stars. Pleasant conversation flowed smoothly. We had a lot of laughs. He was telling me a story about how he'd reacted to something at work when I jokingly said, "You need Jesus!"

"Jesus don't mean anything to me," he threw back at me. Taken aback, I was still for a minute before asking how that was possible. He let me know that while his family goes to church, they don't believe in Jesus. I sat silently for a few minutes before changing the subject. Of course, his response kept playing in my head.

For a couple of days, I held back from asking the hard questions, but finally, I asked, "What are we going to do now?

We don't believe in the same things, so how can we continue with a relationship?"

He told me that I could convert, and we would be great; nothing had to change. However, everything changed. I believe in Jesus. He is God's only begotten son sent here to die for all sins. How could I act like I never knew Him and that His sacrifice meant nothing?

I thought that guy was everything that I needed, but our beliefs were not the same and we were not equally yoked. So, I ended the relationship. Making the decision was hard, but I could save my soul and that's worth way more than any 'happily ever after.'

Respond Here

Think back to a time when you put a relationship with someone before your relationship with God? What happened to make you rethink and brought you back to putting God first?

_____

_____

_____

_____

If you are/were waiting do/did you trust God would bring you a life mate, and are/were you afraid to wait?

_____

_____

_____

_____

Affirmation

I will never settle, nor will I turn my back on my God. I will wait on the Lord and trust His timing.

It's Praying Time

Dear Heavenly Father, I come to You with an open heart. I know that my relationship with You is more significant than any relationship with a man. You showed Your love for me, even before I came to this world, so I could never turn my back on You. You are my shield, defender, and healer, and I trust you with my life. I know You will send my life-mate one day, and I pray that I can allow Your perfect love to cast out any fears or doubts in that relationship.

In Jesus' Name, Amen

TIME TO FORGIVE YOURSELF

Paulette Jaminson

There is therefore now no condemnation to them

which are in Christ Jesus, who walk not after the flesh,

but after the Spirit.

Romans 1:1 (KJV)

One of the most challenging things many people struggle with in life is forgiving themselves. God is faithful and will forgive us of all sins. This simple statement requires a massive responsibility for us to receive. We tend to marinate in our mistakes; they become daily items on the menu.

When a person has done wrong, the taste of guilt and shame is very bitter. Yet, a person will eat it anyway, convincing themselves it should be on the plate.

I had my first daughter at the age of sixteen and struggled with guilt for many years. My parents considered this a big disgrace to our family. Though I was blessed with a healthy baby, I felt such guilt and shame, unworthy of any good thing in my life.

I could not forgive myself for hurting my parents, nor could I look them in their eyes. The shame consumed me and lasted for many years.

One day in my prayer time, I heard the Lord say, "If you have surrendered all to me, why haven't you forgiven yourself? I forgave you, and your parents have forgiven you. Let yourself off the hook today; say farewell. This experience is a story you can tell."

I listened to the Lord and groomed my daughter into a beautiful young lady. My daughter has become a minister, and our family is very proud of her.

True, sometimes we don't do our best, but we serve God, who loves us unconditionally. He said He would always be with us.

So, no matter what happens in your life, don't allow guilt and shame to weigh you down. God is telling you, "Let yourself off the hook"; experience the sweetness in life again. Right now – today is the time to forgive yourself!

Respond Here

Write the things that are currently weighing heavy on your heart. Give each of them to God and then say goodbye to them forever.

_____

_____

_____

_____

Think of a time you did not forgive yourself. How did it make you feel, and what did you do to move from that state of mind?

_____

_____

_____

_____

Affirmation

I release myself from the heavy shame, guilt, and burden of my past so I can step into my future with a positive mind.

It's Praying Time

Lord, I give You all the glory and all the praise. I am grateful for this new beginning to forgive myself and start a powerful journey based on your unfailing promise to forgive me of all my repented sins. I am centered in Christ, so, therefore, there is no more condemnation in my heart or my soul. Lord, I stand on Your word that says if I resist the devil, he will flee from me. Lord, help me to do what I have committed to do.

In Jesus' Name, Amen

UNSTOPPABLE

Dr. Annette West

As you come to him, the living Stone—rejected by

humans but chosen by God and precious to him

— you also, like living stones, are being built

into a spiritual house to be a holy priesthood,

offering spiritual sacrifices acceptable

to God through Jesus Christ.

I Peter 2:4-5 (NIV)

The Word of the Lord is precious yet often is rejected by man. Looking at the scripture for this devotion, I was reminded that people must develop a yearning for Christ.

As we walk and live in Christ, we are being built for this. What is this? It is the predestined plan of the Lord for our lives. God brought Jesus to this earth with a purpose to set the captives free. He asked the Father to take the suffering away during that plan. Yet, Christ endured fulfilling His purpose.

There is a plan for everyone's life. Looking back over my life and thinking things over, the early road was tough. Yet, as I look back, obstacles were everywhere, but I overcame them. Why? Because everything I endured built me for this. No, I don't believe that all I endured was in God's plan because life has 'ebb and flow,' and the chosen roads were of my choosing.

My family and environment formed my early years. However, once I moved to a new environment and a spiritual relationship in Christ, things changed. Offering spiritual sacrifices to the Lord became my reality, living God's predestined plan for a greater purpose beyond what I initially understood.

The greater purpose is to be an ambassador of Christ; this is what we are built for in this life. We are built for this – to be Ambassadors of Christ! Shaped into a living temple, and the Spirit of God dwells within. How do we know this? We know because God has entrusted us with the gospel, and we must go forward to share it with the world.

Respond Here

From reading the devotion, list three points that stood out to you and how you can apply them to your life?

_____

_____

_____

_____

Think about and write how you are unstoppable because of your relationship with Christ.

_____

_____

_____

_____

_____

_____

Affirmation

I am designed for a grand purpose, unstoppable, and able to accomplish all that He predestined for my life.

It's Praying Time

Oh Lord, my God, I love You. Thank You for all that I've endured, as it has made me the vessel I am today. I have the strength in You to make it through every situation and circumstance that comes in my life. I have learned so much about my familial ties. Thank You for my new birth in You. Daily I am being built up to serve and glorify Your Name. I am Your ambassador and will go forward and shine for You in all that I do, say, and be. I am built for this.

In Jesus' Name, Amen

WHO'S GOT YOU COVERED?

Dan Barton

Jerusalem, Jerusalem, you who kill the prophets

and stone those sent to you, how often I have longed

to gather your children together, as a hen gathers her chicks under her

wings, and you were not willing.

Look, your house is left to you desolate.

Matthew 23:37-38 (NIV)

There it was again, that unmistakable sound of footsteps coming down the third-floor hallway of our home in Lansing, Michigan. Every night from the ages of three to ten, an unscripted play took place in the Barton household. Both players in this nightly ritual performed their role to perfection.

There never was a script written or a choreographer consulted. The precision was unmistakable. I would toss and turn and unwittingly mangle my bedding. The sensation of frostbite gripping my entire body woke me up. I would muster the strength and yell with enthusiasm, "Come cover me up!" Dad always came and silently brought comfort and covers.

Several years passed and I figured out how to disentangle myself and rearrange my bedding. One night I woke up with a familiar dilemma, but a new idea entered my thought processes. "I wonder if he would still come?" I put my father to the test.

My parents awoke to an almost forgotten cry for help to waft through the early morning silence one more time. "Come cover me up!"

Thoughts flooded my twelve-year-old mind. What emotions have my unnecessary, disrespectful disturbance of his peace riled up in my devoted father? Would he come, or would he shout back, "Do it yourself!"

My father passed my test without ever knowing he was on trial. He always was! I never again wondered if Dad would be there for me in times of trouble.

Just like this example, Jesus longs to cover and shield His children. He protects His children from the plans of the enemy. When one follows Jesus they don't have to put him to the test. He already passed the ultimate test when He shed His blood on the cross. He gave His life to pay the debt so His children can be free.

Respond Here

Identify and list three areas of weakness in your life where you have been exposed to an enemy attack.

a. _____

_____

b. _____

_____

c. _____

_____

List three ways you can commit to spending time every day.

a. _____

_____

b. _____

_____

c. _____

_____

Affirmation

God thank You for covering my vulnerabilities and keeping me covered.

It's Praying Time

Lord Jesus, I come to You again realizing that my failure and arrogance has one more time put me at odds with You and Your plans for me and my life. I have gotten careless and allowed other people and selfish motives to distract me from Your purpose. I ask You to forgive me and "Come Cover Me Up." Help me to remember You, "I have longed to gather your children together, as a hen gathers her chicks under her wings." I need You to shelter me in a way that no one or nothing else can. I acknowledge You as both my Savior and Lord.

In Jesus' Name, Amen

MEET THE AUTHORS
of the
Volume 1
Centered in Christ
Devotional
Steadfast and Immovable

Dr. Dan Barton

 Dan Barton has been married to his beautiful bride since 1979. Dan and Kathy have two living adult children who have given them six grandchildren. He began working in a furniture hardware factory while in college. After nine years there, Dan went to graduate school, where he received his Master's in Pastoral Ministry and later his Doctor of Pastoral Counseling. He pastored in six states for over 35 years. During his pastoral ministry, he also served as Chaplain in five hospices and has been a hospital chaplain for more than 15 decades.

Author's Contact:

DanBarton.me
DRB@DanBarton.me
DRBpoet@gmail.com
AndSatanLaughed.com
DRB@AndSatanLaughed.com

Neva Brooks

 Neva Brooks has a God ordained purpose to serve. She is committed to empowering women to move from a place of conflict to places of confidence and clarity.

For more than 35 years she has served as a Registered Nurse, specializing in Behavioral and Mental Wellness.

She is a mother, grandmother, and Godmother. Currently, ministers in her local church, and is a licensed ceremonial minister and officiant in the state of Missouri.

She birthed the ministry Diamonds Sharpens Diamonds™ which is a ministry empowering each other. She is the CEO of Diamond Sharp Coaching, LLC.

Author's Contact:

DiamondSharpCoach@gmail.com

www.DiamondSharpCoach.com

Cynthia Crawford

 Cynthia E. Crawford is a child of God, wife, mother, and the CEO of Authentic Existence®. She encourages all to boldly reflect the light of the "Son," Jesus Christ. She calls this being a Bold Full Moon™. This mission was birthed from her life journey, full of worldly success, that left her in bondage to a world in which she didn't fit. She strengthens faith fitness in others like her, for freedom through Christ, by inspiring them to open the eyes of their hearts, with her symbolic jewelry and unique products as visual reminders to affirm the Word.

Author's Contact:

boldfullmoon.com

info@boldfullmoon.com

Sybil E. Davis-Highdale

 Sybil E. Davis-Highdale, a co-founder of Lost Sheep Cavalry Ministries International, which began as a Motorcycle Ministry, considers herself blessed to be of service. She serves in short-term missions considering Cambodia her second home. The experiences from being a Disaster Crisis Chaplain and volunteer lead in several non-profit organizations have strengthened her mission. Her mission is to enlighten, ignite, motivate, and nurture communities of loving, faith-filled, and service-focused saints in creative ways to follow their divine purpose without conformity, living by the motto, "For to me, to live is Christ and to die is gain," (Philippians 1:21, NIV).

Author Contact

LostSheepCavalry.com

https://www.facebook.com/sanctifiedsista.davishighdale

Camelia Grannum

 Camelia Grannum is a gift designed to make a difference in the lives of everyone she encounters. Growing up she dreamed of making a difference in the lives of others. She has spent years of her life learning from her life challenges, experiences, and mistakes. She has seen tremendous growth over the years. Her goal is to exceed her growth potential and become her best self while impacting lives through positivity and uplifting others. She is a work in progress.

She believes that our lives reflect the choices we make. According to scripture, "We reap what we sow."

We should do our best to make wise choices to avoid unnecessary suffering and learn from our mistakes and those of others.

Author Contact

Chooseorlose2021@gmail.com

Ccameliagrannum.wearelegalshield.ca

Noreen Hobson

 Noreen Hobson is The Visionary Implementer. She is a woman of Faith who loves God. Noreen is a wife and a mother of 2 children. She is a Singer, Speaker and serves in Youth Ministry. She is a Certified Project Management Professional (PMP) and Certified Christian Life Coach. Noreen enjoys helping Christians discover and develop their God-given potential into a Visionary Goal Action Plan, to Launch Out by Faith and Achieve Good Success.

Noreen believes in God's Word that I can do all things through Christ who strengthens me. She encourages you to apply your Faith daily with God.

Author Contact

NoreenHobson.com

Paulette Jaminson

 Paulette Jaminson is a sought-after motivational speaker, counselor, coach, and a powerful prayer warrior. She was born in London, England the second child of Lascelles and Dorothy Jaminson. She is a mother of four daughters. She is the founder and Pastor of House of Revival Ministries in New Britain CT., and the founder of Soldiers of Survival, an empowerment support group. Her passion is birthed through her pain and struggles in life, to be the salt and the light as Jesus commanded. She allows the Holy Spirit to work through her changing the lives of many.

Author Contact

Facebook: Paulette Jaminson

Instagram: pastor_paulettejaminson

Website: www.refreshedandrevived.org

Lekeisha Mosley

Lekeisha Mosley is a woman on purpose. For over 15 years, she has been a Business Identity Strategist. Her target is to show you how to reset and recharge your goals for women with mental illness and reset your plans with positive inspiration and happiness! Author, Coach, Mental Illness Advocate, The Inspiration Happiness Cultivator, and owner of MyIdentityDrivenLife, LLC.

Author Contact

www.lekeishamosley.com

thelekeishamosleyshow@mail.com

Pablo Murillo

 Pablo Murillo is a High-Performance Mindset Coach/Professional Speaker for Yenesis Leadership, Mira, Mira, Mira!! He was born in Nicaragua and grew up during the Sandinista Revolution of the 1970's. He learned early in his childhood what "Power of the People" really meant. He came to the USA in the late 1980's and after learning English attended UCLA. He is a public speaker, has developed leaders for over 25 years and the founder of Yenesis Leadership Trainings assisting organizations and individuals to increase their leadership skills. Yenesis Leadership is created as an avenue to do what he is passionate about which is to see the light bulb turn on in a person's eyes when they realize there is a whole new world, of self-awareness, self-discovery, and advancement skills before them.

Author Contact

My website: www.yenesisleadership.com

Email: info@yenesisleadership.com

Tuesday Payne

 Tuesday Payne is a woman who believes that all things are possible when you put your trust in God. For the past 15 years, she has made it her mission to help the elderly and less fortunate. Tuesday believes that giving of herself is the way to achieve her heart's desire which is, helping others. She has not allowed health issues to deter that mission but to motivate her because she believes there is always someone worse off. Tuesday does a Monday devotional in Living Word and a Wednesday Devotional in The Word Fellowship International. She manages to raise funds for Bibles to send to Kenya and helps with several of Dr. Annette West's missions. She truly sees an opportunity in every situation.

Author's Contact

tpayne1599@yahoo.com

https://www.linkedin.com/in/tuesday-payne-3b3b0255

Janice Rock

Janice Rock is a native of South Carolina. She's an Educator and expert in Ministry Leadership. Janice is the owner of Bridge Consulting Firm where she's an advocate for veterans and the disabled. She is the CEO of Royaltwear T-Shirt Designs, LLC. She has a degree in Education and Innovation, Organization Management and Business. She is certified in Online Teaching and Learning, and Entrepreneurship.

She has a heart for singles' and has invested years working to help them process through areas of brokenness. Her hobbies consist of watching action-packed movies, reading, and empowering others to obtain their purpose in life.

Her favorite quote: "Start before you're ready." Steven Pressfield

Author Contact

Store: Janice-rock.onlineweb.shop

Jacqueline Smith

 Jacqueline Smith is a woman of wisdom. She has been an advisor to women, men, and teenagers for over 25 years. She has a mandate to empower people by giving them keys that will unlock the mind, bring healing to the soul through God's revelation and wisdom. She continues to remain teachable, living a life of prayer to fulfil God's perfect plan for her life. She ministers internationally, as well as locally, traveling and speaking as God leads. Her moto is "every woman needs a woman." "She is being exactly who God called her to be, an ambassador for His name's sake while functioning in the office of the Apostle."

Author Contact

1FreshOilMinistries@gmail.com

https://awepublishing.bigcartel.com

www.GodsAwe.com

AnointedWomenEmpowered@gmail.com

Dr. Irene Watson

 Dr. Irene E. Watson is a born-again believer who loves serving people, seeing lives changed and witnessing the Word of God to the lost. She enjoys operating in an atmosphere of teaching, learning, and sharing. She is the Founder of the Hope Empowerment Project and ARISE Women's Fellowship. Both organizations are noted for uplifting and training women of all ages, ethnicities, occupations, and education. She is a Certified Christian Counselor, Self-development Coach, and Mentor who loves to encourage and bring inspiration to hopeless situations.

Authors Contact

dr.irenewatson@gmail.com

irenewatson373@gmail.com

Dr. Annette West

Dr. Annette West is a woman on purpose. For over 35 years, it has been her goal to find ways to better care for her mind, body, and spiritual walk. As she grows, sharing and empowering others' growth is always her goal. She believes that when we learn to maintain an optimal level of wellness, we are aligned better with God's ways. She logistically supports missions in Kakamega, Kenya, Nigeria, and India.

She always shares that "she is the visible manifestation of His invisible presence" we must have the SONshine always flowing.

Authors Contact

GinQKBoost.com

JATNE Publishing.org

DrAnnetteWestMinistries.org

Nikki West

 Nikki West is a mother, daughter, sister, friend, and most of all, Woman of God. She has a natural love for children and has devoted 10+ years to being a "second parent" to many. Nikki has a Bachelor of Science degree in Business and is currently working as a web page designer and virtual assistant.

In addition, Nikki is a Teaching Assistant, and has started a new business, Unfiltered Society, with her best friend. It is a clothing brand that focuses mainly on motivating others to be Unique. Unbothered. Unapologetic. In other words, comfortable being their true selves.

Authors Contact

Email: nswest81@gmail.com

Phone: (803) 357-3690

Centered in Christ Devotional Project

Joining the JATNE team of contributing authors is an opportunity for aspiring or seasoned book authors. You will be able to add your co-authored book to your shelf or another book to your marketing toolbox.

Join our next devotional project. Each publication is written and aimed to assist readers in gaining a more robust understanding of scriptures and learning ways of life application through reading stories of contributing authors.

If interested, please know you will be asked to submit

- a non-refundable, but transferable, $75 registration fee is required to be considered for the devotional project. The fee will, also, hold your spot for the upcoming devotional publication of JATNE, if accepted. We will request brief sample of your writing about the theme and will provide you with feedback.
- a professional black and white headshot jpg photo.
- a brief biographical sketch of 50-75 words.

We look forward to having you join the growing number of JATNE authors. Reach us at Jatnepublishing@mail.com

Write – Writer – Writing

JATNE Publishing works with Christian, faith-based, inspirational individuals eager to write and publish books with messages designed for life application through alignment of Scripture to strengthen the reader's spiritual walk.

Are you already a writer or want to become one? We will guide you to through the steps to prepare a manuscript and be ready to publish and launch your book in six months. You also can complete your book by taking part in a JATNE boot camp. You will engage with other writers to learn or review the writing process and complete your book.

If you've been thinking about writing a book, publishing as an individual author, it's time. If you are ready to pull thought from your mind and get it on paper, JATNE Publishing is here to assist you in getting your message out there.

For more information on publishing options, please email us at jatnepublishing@mail.com

It's all about Faith – Family – Flourish, to move to the next level!

List of the Devotional Scriptures

Other Books by *JATNE* Publishing

Bible Break (2021)

Marriage Connection Making it Work (2021)

Wait Trust Gods Timing for a Mate (2021)

A Mind Created By Love, Hate, Betrayal (2020)

Centered in Christ (2020)

Holistic Wellness Mind Body Spirit (2019)

Holistic Wellness Mind Body Spirit (journal) (2019)

23-Day Devotional The Book of Isaiah (2018)

Jesus the Path to Victorious Living (2017)

Living Words of Encouragement Vol 2 (2016)

Living Words of Encouragement Vol 1 (2006)

Basic Biblical Building Blocks (2002)

Entrepreneurship: Making Money God's Way in God's Time (2000)

Made in USA - North Chelmsford, MA
1287111_9781732026070
10.28.2021 1510